to be full to the point of brea
to break open or apart sudden

Anxiety

an uncomfortable feeling of
futur

RELEAS

provide you the t
decrease your an

© 2021 Keisha McDonald-Griffin
ISBN:978-1-955234-04-7
All rights reserved. No part of this publication may be reproduced, distributed, or transmitted in any form or by any means, including photocopying, recording, or other electronic or mechanical methods, without the prior written permission of the publisher, except in the case of brief quotations embodied in critical reviews and certain other noncommercial uses permitted by copyright law.

For permission requests, contact Keisha McDonald-Griffin at amourlegacipublishing@gmail.com.

This is a work of fiction. Any resemblance to actual events or persons, living or dead, is entirely coincidental.
1st editionBook Design: Keisha McDonald-Griffin
Production: AmourLegaci Publishing
Editing: Keisha McDonald
Illustrations: Web designs
Publisher: AmourLegaci Publishing
To order: maddtherapy.com, Amazon.com (ebook), Barnes & Noble, Amourlegacipublishing.com
Author Website: Amourlegacipublishing.com
Printed in United States of America

You are in the right place if...

Your feeling anxious about doing something

You live with an anxiety disorder

Need to calm down quickly

Wants immediate relief with long term effects

Keisha McDonald MS, MA, LPC, CATP

About the Author

Therapy is a process of growth and self-discovery, and can be experienced in various forms. I promote behavioral transformation by encouraging a positive outlook and the adoption of new attitudes and relationships.

I am a therapist who strives to empower others to obtain successful outcomes as they are faced with life challenges. I work with individuals experiencing anxiety, depression, self esteem, foster care related issues and child and adolescent trauma.

I operate a practice called MADD Therapy in Michigan. I also work with clients through Renewed Counseling in Michigan. I have extensive knowledge & experience working with clients and families who are struggling with anxiety, depression, adjustment disorders, foster care related issues and child trauma. I also have additional training in child and adolescent trauma, cognitive behavioral therapy, dialectical behavioral therapy and trauma focused cognitive behavioral therapy.

I use expressive arts in addition to elements of cognitive behavioral, motivational interviewing, solution focused, mindfulness and other therapies to help clients.

maddtherapy

Table of Contents

1	What is Anxiety?
3	Thought blocking
7	Anxiety relief
10	Get Active
16	Kids & Anxiety
20	Achieving the CALM
25	Skills
55	Recap

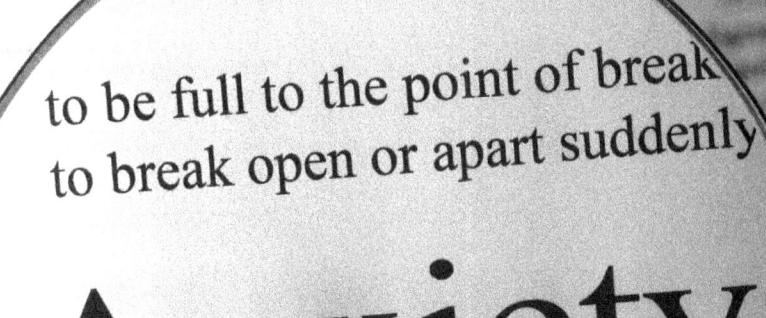

to be full to the point of break
to break open or apart suddenly

Anxiety

an uncomfortable feeling of ner
or might happen in the future

Anxiety

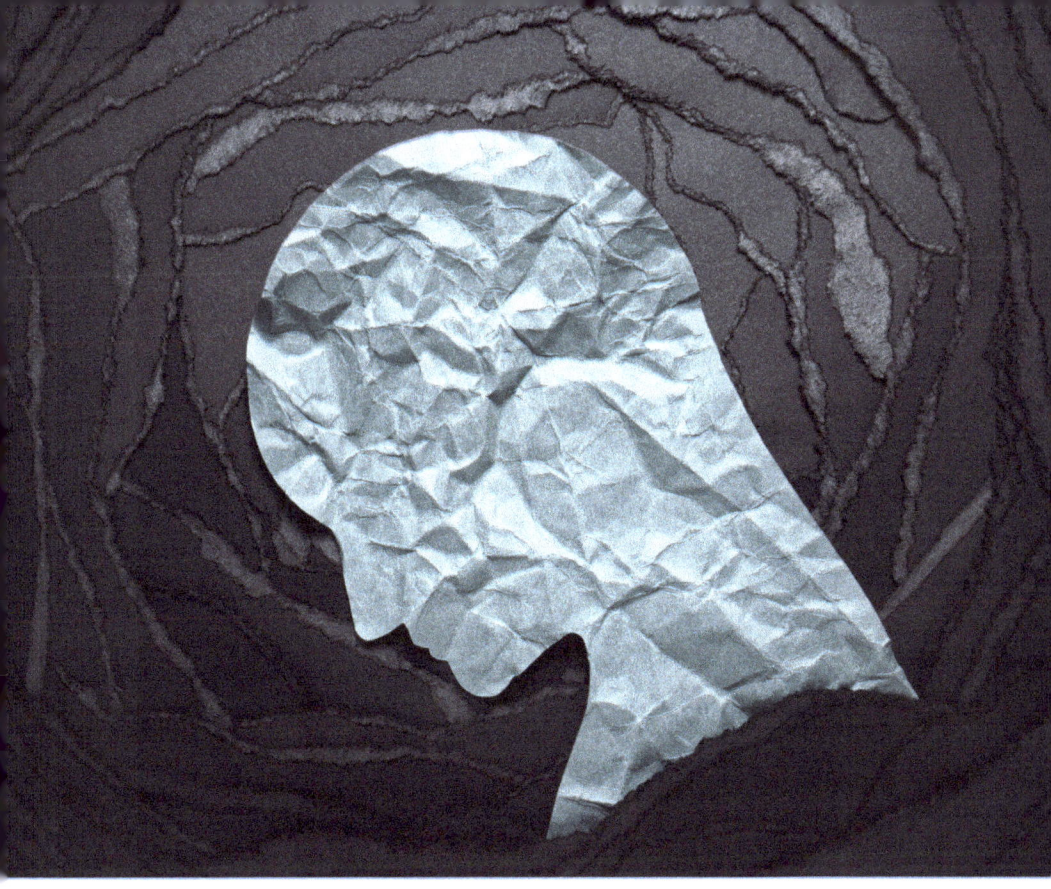

What is Anxiety?

Anxiety is the response of the body under a perceived threat. When you are feeling extremely overwhelmed and full of anxiety there are some things that you can do to help yourself through those moments. "Anxiety is defined as "a state of intense apprehension, uncertainty, and fear resulting from the anticipation of a threatening event or situation, often to a degree that normal physical and psychological functioning is disrupted"(American Heritage Medical Dictionary, 2020)."

Therefore,

Anxiety is an intense feeling of multiple emotions that are overwhelming. Some physical symptoms of what you may feel is emotion overload, muscle tension, headache, dizziness, shakes, heart racing, rapid breathing. Emotional symptoms include restlessness, a sense of impending doom, fear of dying, fear of embarrassment or humiliation, or fear of something terrible happening.

Thought Blocking

Thought blocking is when overwhelming emotions begin to cloud your mind of any and everything that you would like to think about. The overload of emotion causes thought blocking. Thought blocking is when you are not capable of thinking natural normal thoughts. This keeps you from being able to logically think of what to do next or even how to help yourself which sends you into a panic.

This is where the attack of anxiety comes from. The fear the thought blocking caused during your time of natural anxiety has now caused panic.

Anxiety manifests in multiple ways, including fear for the future on a cognitive level muscle tension on a physical level, and situational avoidance on a behavioral level. Anxiety impacts the functioning of an individual, including varying degrees of difficulty in establishing and maintaining interpersonal relationships. Anxiety also persist over time representing ongoing challenges for the many people living with it.

I let go of what I can't change and do my best with what I can.

DECREASE YOUR ANXIETY

The GOAL is FOR YOU...

is to decrease your daily anxiety trouble by 75%.

ANXIETY

An anxiety producing situation leads to uncomfortable symptoms such as worry, fear, a racing heart, sweating, or a feeling of being overwhelmed.

When you feel a sense of anxiety the first thought is to avoid the situation so you can avoid having the feelings associated with it. Avoidance is the uncomfortable symptom that is controlled by the anxiety-producing situation. Some examples of avoiding the situation is the use of drugs to numb the feelings, procrastinating completing a task, choosing to not participate in the situation that is causing the anxiety.

Short-term relief

Short-term relief from anxiety provides an immediate sense of relief. The short term release lessens the symptoms of anxiety but only temporarily.

Long-term relief

Long term anxiety is caused by the symptoms of anxiety worsening due to anxiety being experienced over a long period of time. The brain learns that when the anxiety-producing situation is avoided, the symptoms go away however, symptoms will be worse next time and avoidance will be more likely.

Consider emotions but don't let them take charge. Calming the nervous system is important when you are trying to decrease anxiety. One of the most natural things we do daily and is connected to our nervous system is to breathe. Taking a breath is an important step in decreasing anxiety and is tied to our emotions. We have two responses to anxiety and fear. Our thoughts and bodies speed up.

Breathing

Breathing is essential to bringing balance back to your body when you experience anxiety. FOCUSing on your breathe allows you to bring your attention to the action of breathing. When you are able to focus on breathing you feel the sensations of the belly rising and falling. You are also able to notice the sound of the breath.

✅ Associate breathing with relaxation. Use repetitive words when you exhale and inhale, such as in ......when you inhale and out.....when you exhale. Taking long deep breaths help you to fill your lungs and changes your body posture. During the inhale you feel your low belly expand first, then your ribs, and finally your chest. Do not strain. It takes practice to change the pattern of shallow breathing. Extend the exhale slowly. Make it last as long as possible.

Get ACTIVE

GET ACTIVE (this doesn't mean go excercise)
Being active means to get up and do something. Move around. Be Busy. Being proactive. When dealing with anxiety it is important to actively do things to help decrease the unhealthy anxiety you are experiencing. Being active and intentional about what you do an d how you do it is an important step to decreasing and releasing your excess anxiety.

ACTIVE Ways to decrease your anxiety include:

ACTIVELY Calming anxiety
What do you do to calm your anxiety
Become a capable problem solver. Create a saying to repeat that comforts you while experiencing anxiety. Do not use habitual patterns of overreacting to stress.

ACTIVELY take a walk alone or with a pet. A 30 min walk daily can asssit you in decreasing your anxiety. Active movement can physically, literally and metaphorically get you unstuck. Taking a walk will get you out of the house, get you moving and get you out of your head and away from the anxious thoughts.

ACTIVELY Hydrate
Staying hydrated is a simple way to improve your mental health. Water facilitates the delievery of nutrients to the brain, removes toxins and inflammatory markers, and improves cognitive abilities.

ACTIVELY Excercise
A short burst of heightened physical activity can help get rid of nervous energy.

ACTIVELY Think of comfort
Anxiety can make you feel isolated , even when you are not physically alone. Think of comforting places or people when you begin to feel overwhelmed and draw inspiration from them.

ACTIVELY try new things
Change your routine can help you nor be so anxious. By setting limits on what you do and how long you do it can help you gain a sense of control and help you focus on the task and not the anxiety. Try setting timer for 25 minutes followed by a 5 minute break. During that break actively do a grounding techniques or practice mindfulness. Repeat the cycle 3-4 times, then take a much deserved 15-20 minute break making sure to do self care during that time.

ACTIVELY be mindful
Sitting in silence can help you gather yourself and find your peace. Take a few moments to sit in silence, take a few deep breaths and intentionally allow yourself to just be in this moment.

ACTIVELY Declutter
It is true that your environment usually reflects your mind. A messy space indicates a messy mind. Tidying up or organizing is a active coping skill you can count on to help clear your mind and space.

ACTIVELY focus on your reality
What is a your reality? We often are looking for answers to our questions through others. However, someone else's reality is not your reality which will produce a different answer and result to your question. Take a moment and think about what is true for you in this moment. What is your reality and how do you navigate fixing it? There most like are many things you have not considered that are causing challenges for you. Take off the rose colored glasses and realize life is throwing you a curve ball and it's time for you to get in the game.

ACTIVELY have FUN
When you are feeling low, have lack of motivation or just don't want to be bothered due to how we are feeling, these are the times it's important to not isolate yourself. Isolation causes loneliness, feelings of despair and hopelessness. Get out, make plans with fun people to boost your mood. Just being active and making plans can boost your mood. It's ok to chicken out and not go, but continue to try to make it out of that door.

ACTIVELY ACCEPT your ANXIETY
We all have feelings and guess what? Your feelings has feelings! Your anxiety wants to be acknowledged. When we choose to ignore anxiety it just gets worse. Once you learn to accept that anxiety is a part of your life you can begin to decrease the unhealthy amount of anxiety you are experiencing. Sometimes it takes more work on your part than what's others have to do but that's because your anxiety is yours. It's ok to let go of the need to control outcomes. This leads to greater acceptance of your circumstances.

Remembering that as uncomfortable as your ANXIETY is your track record for overcoming the symptoms is probably close to 100 percent.

Kids & Anxiety

Kids experience anxiety too. Many situations produce anxiety for children. School, home, relationships, test, social situations, even chores can cause anxiety. Being aware of your child's movements and activities will help you better help them when they are experiencing anxiety.

Communication is one of the best ways to help a child decrease their anxiety. Talking to your child will not only provide you with information about why your child is anxious, it will help your child's anxiety subside. Talking to someone is a coping skill that helps to decrease anxiety almost immediately. The conversation does not have to be about anxiety at all. Just having a conversation will **HELP** your child decrease their anxiety.

When kids are anxious, they often experienced the acute stress response known as fight, flight, or freeze, in which the bodies sympathetic nervous system releases adrenaline and noradrenalin, increasing heart rate, blood pressure, and breathing rate.

Kids respond to the fight flight or freeze in different ways. Some scream, shake, or run away, while others make it quiet, act silly, clean, or have a tantrum. During these times it is difficult to figure out what the child needs. Many times not even the child knows what they need in that moment. Your child will not be able to understand in that moment what to do, what they need, or how to control their own behavior until they can step out of that fight, flight, or freeze mode.

You can achieve the Calm in kids. Here's how

Achieving the CALM

Some of the ways that you can help your child with anxiety and achieve a calm demeanor are things that you typically would do on a normal day but in this case you are intentionally utilizing these techniques to help your child decrease their anxiety and calm them selves.

1. **Stimulate the Vagus nerve.** What is that? The Vagus nerve is located on both sides of the voice box, these nerves can send a signal to the brain that states it is not under attack. The way that it will send the nerve is by actively utilizing it. Encouraging a child to chew gum, sing or hum, breathe slowly Utilizing breathing techniques included or even eating a piece of dark chocolate could help achieve the calm and decrease the anxiety.
2. **Create a ritual.** Creating a ritual says that there is a routine in place when things happen which causes the child to feel safer in that moment. Rituals can be anchors of stability and can help an anxious child approach and anxiety provoking situation with a greater confidence in a sense of control. Some rituals can include reading their favorite book, playing their favorite song, or doing jumping jacks. A physical ritual may be more reliable as it

does not depend on the presence of other objects such as a music player or having a book available.

3. **Have a plan.** Anxiety is unpredictable. For a child having an unpredictable situation occur is stressful and can potentially be Traumatic to that child. Discussing with your child in advance what helps them when they are feeling stressed or feeling nervous can help you develop a plan with your child on what to do in the event they are feeling this way. Doing activities that children like to do helps to decrease anxiety. Some of the activities you may want to add to your plan are coloring, stringing beads, playing with an object like a fidget toy or even getting outside to do some deep breathing or walking or even playing with a pet.

4. **Encourage breathing.** There are many breathing exercises that children can use to help them decrease their anxiety. Blowing bubbles, blowing into a pinwheel, blowing out fingertip candles, whistling, or breathing in for a count of three, holding for three, and breathing out for three can help as can breathing in through the nose and out through the mouth. There are diagrams of breathing exercises in the appendix.

5. **Name the feelings.** When a child is in fight, flight, or freeze mode it also causes thought blocking for that child. What this means is your child is unable to think of what to do to calm themselves, decrease the anxiety, or even tell you what it is that they need. Allowing your child the time to calm themselves through deep breathing or another coping skills can help them be able to name their feelings. naming the feelings the child is experiencing, can help children gain a sense of control and eventually calm.

6. **Imagine.** Helping your child to imagine a calm state will also help to decrease anxiety. many children live within their imagination and have many safe places in their Imaginative state. Calmly tell your child to imagine a safe place, a place that they have created in their mind, a place that they would like to go or the place that they have been and feel it is safe for them. This technique is like guided imagery. Guided imagery is a form of focused relaxation that helps create harmony between the mind and body. It is a way of focusing your imagination to create calm, peaceful images in your mind, thereby providing a "mental escape."

7. **Laugh.** Laughter can significantly reduce anxiety. It provides distraction, relaxes your muscles, and releases endorphins that can help combat stress. Hope your child is out of an anxious state just by making a joke. "Why did the chicken cross the road? I don't know chickens aren't usually on the road."

8. **Exercise.** Exercising is activating. Active movement helps the muscles and joints and it also increases the focus and attention to help you center yourself. Doing push-ups against the wall, running a vacuum cleaner, climbing a jungle gym, or pulling a wagon can help a kid calm down and regulate their emotions.

Also, be sure to check out our books Parenting the Storm: A Parent's Guide to Helping Your Child Regulate and I Am Not My Anxiety (for Kids) — both available on Amazon and Barnes & Noble.

SKILLS

So what do you do?

We all suffer from a normal amount of anxiety. That normal amount clues you into when things are wrong or if you should make a different choice because what you are feeling just doesn't sit well with you. However, some suffer from an over abundance of anxiety which causes difficulty in daily living activities.

Anxiety is closely related to depression and is one of many depression symptoms experienced. Severe anxiety is a risk factor for suicide & suicidal ideation. If you are experiencing either of these please get an assessment completed by a mental health professional.

#1

Consult a therapist.

Psychology Today

This site allows you to seek out counselors in your area that would be helpful to you, for you and you can view their profile before booking an appointment.

Psychologytoday.com

Psychology Today

Your Insurance Carrier

Your insurance carrier

Most insurances can refer you to a counselor to assist you with your needs. Call the number on the back of your insurance card and inquire about counseling services.

Your Doctor's office

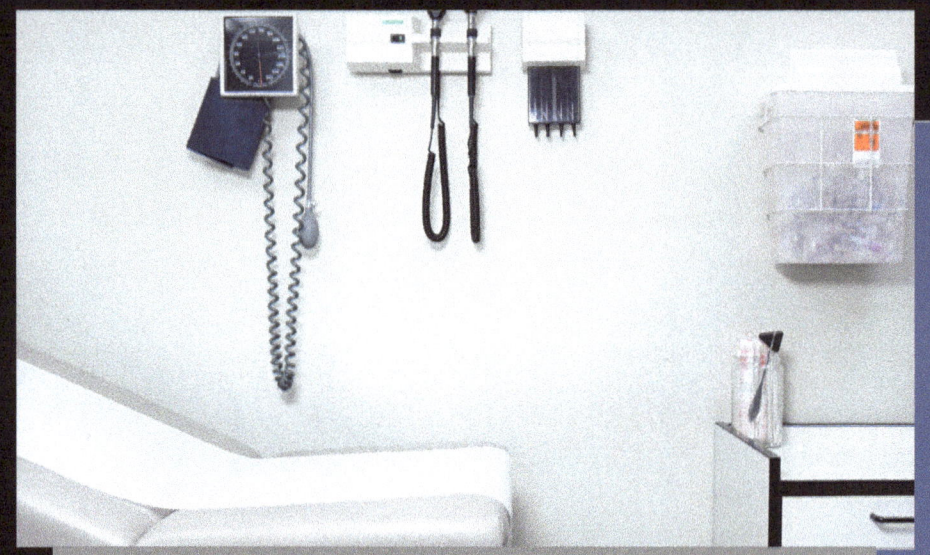

Your doctor's office
Most doctor's offices have referrals to counselors in the area you may be able to reach out to for services. Contact them today and inquire about referrals to counselors in your area.

988 | SUICIDE & CRISIS LIFELINE
24/7 CALL, TEXT, CHAT

1-800-273-8255

This lifeline will not only assist you with brief counseling services to help you in the moment but they can also provide referral information for counselors in your area.

Ask a Friend

Reach out for Support
This option requires you to talk to someone about how you are feeling and will lead you to referrals and support you are seeking.

Daily Anxiety Tools

Tools

There are daily tools that can help with anxiety and practicing the tools daily will equip you to be able to handle when the attack of anxiety happens before it happens.

Acknowledgment

Acknowledge your feelings, acknowledge the things that are making you feel overwhelmed, acknowledge the things that are extremely intense for you. A lot of times we tell ourselves not to feel things because we have other things to do or we don't have time for these feelings. All things want acknowledgement. It is ok for you to feel how you feel, they are your feelings and that is something no-one can take away from you.

Say, "I acknowledge that I feel this way and it is okay. My feelings are my feelings."

Acknowledgment

Once you've acknowledged your feelings then you can move onto actively grounding yourself.

Active Grounding

- Grounding yourself is really like placing yourself in the here and now. We typically operate in the past or the future. A lot of our thoughts and actions are rooted from past things things that have happened in the past or things that we believe will happen in the future.

- Active Grounding brings you into the present moment where you're able to realize that you are ok in that moment. Your focus shifts to what is around you currently.

Active Grounding techniques can be done in any place. Active grounding is the act of you physically doing something to bring yourself more present. Many grounding techniques are mindfulness techniques but the active grounding allows you to focus your attention on an activity rather than trying to be mindful in a moment of fear and chaos.

3 & 1

This grounding technique requires you to choose 3 colors and 1 shape.
You then take the chosen color (ex: RED) and you name everything that is red in the room or around you.

The key is to name those things OUT LOUD. Verbally say those things you see.

When there is nothing else red now name everything that is (ex: GREEN) name those things OUT LOUD. When there is nothing else green
Now name everything that is (ex: BLUE) name those things OUT LOUD. When there is nothing else blue
Now name everything that is in the shape of a (ex: rectangle) name every rectangle you see OUT LOUD.

3 & 1

Active Grounding

It is very important that you verbalizes things out loud. This is the active part of grounding. As you are naming things your anxiety level is decreasing and you are now able to think better because thought blocking is no longer an issue.

Your mind is clear of the things that was causing anxiety and you are now present and in the room with those things that are those colors and those shapes.

5 Senses Grounding

For this grounding technique, you will focus on your 5 senses. Most of us have 5 senses we rely on daily. This technique forces you to focus on those senses to bring you into the here and now. Look around the room or place you are in and verbally call out things that are connected to your 5 senses.

First you call out 5 things you can see with your eyes (sense #1).

Next call out 4 things you can feel (sense #2).

Now call out 3 things you can hear (sense #3).

Now call out 2 things you can smell (sense #4).

Lastly call out 1 thing you can taste (sense #5).

5-4-3-2-1

5 Senses Grounding

Many times if you are experiencing anxiety you have been crying and some of your senses are difficult to use such as your sense of smell and taste.

In those instances you would name things that you wish you could smell or taste.

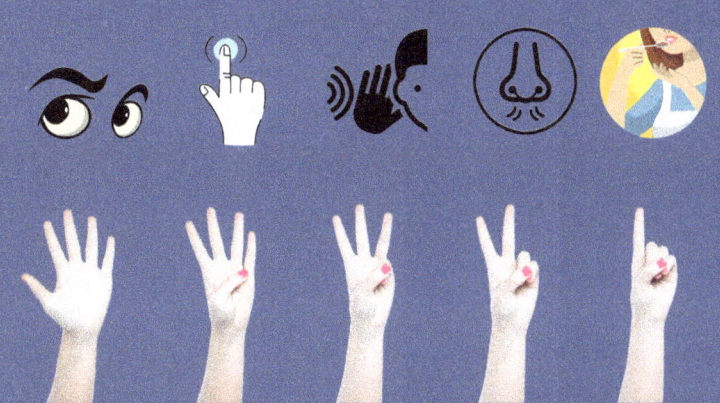

#3

Coping Strategies

Now that you have come to be in your present moment and are grounded most of your overwhelming feelings have dissipated or decreased.

This is the time you use coping skills . Coping skills are things we all do to distract ourselves from things. We do this daily. Our bodies automatically do things to protect us from various emotions on a daily basis. You may use coping skills and not even realize it.

Coping skills can be anything that helps you to move on from something negative and distracts you from those emotions.

It could be journalling, taking a walk, taking a shower, listening to music, watching television, watching your favorite episode of something or playing a video game.

Coping skills help you to better deal with the situation however, because you have grounded yourself already the coping skills you use will be more effective.

TRY THIS

- Design PositiveSelf-Talk Self-talk is engaging in thoughts that will encourage you in making it through the anxious times you experience.
- Read & Repeat positive affirmations
- Aromatherapy (smell something pleasant and inhale deeply)
- Deep breathing

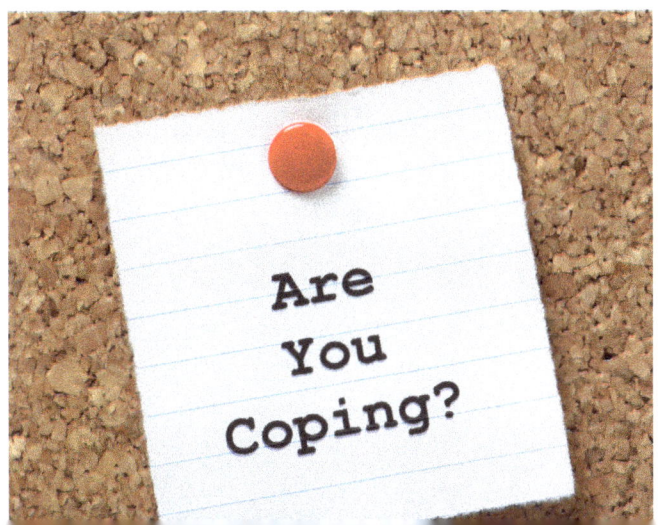

SELF CARE

Now, that you have acknowledged your feelings, grounded yourself, decreased your anxiety and done a coping skill; it is time to reward yourself for being intentional about how you cared for yourself through the exercise of decreasing your anxiety.

The steps you take do not have to be a long drawn out process. It can take five minutes to go through the steps to help your anxiety level decrease so that you can move on with the rest of your day being productive.

What are your Self-care activities?

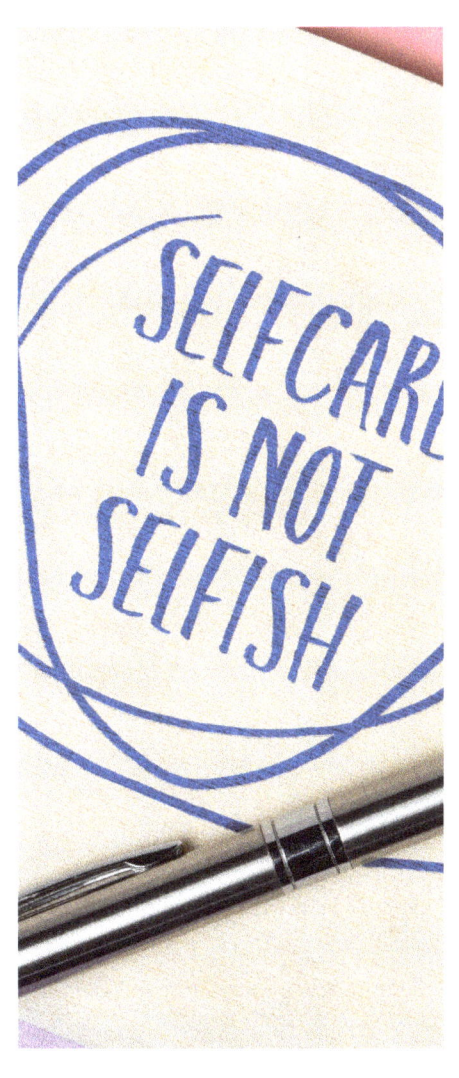

The key to decreasing your anxiety is to use your tools. Use these tools daily. In fact use them multiple times in a day so that you are use to doing what's best for you in those intense moments of panic and fear. The tools help you to reset yourself so that you can be better equipped to deal with those intense emotions when they come around again.

The KEY

Self-care is a lot like coping skills. Many of the things we do to cope are similar things we do for enjoyment and relaxation.

Self-care or things that you enjoy doing that brings you joy ,puts a smile on your face and makes your heart flutter can be something as simple as eating your favorite comfort food, taking that longer than normal hot shower, taking a hot relaxing bubble bath, taking a walk, enjoy listening to that music, having a mani/pedi day and just taking a few moments out of your day to do these things.

RECAP

01 STEP 1 — ACKNOWLEDGE YOUR FEELINGS

02 STEP 2 — ACTIVELY GROUND YOURSELF

03 STEP 3 — COPING SKILL

04 STEP 4 — SELF CARE

05 STEP 5 — REPEAT as often as needed

RESOURCES

Additional things you can do to assist you in your time of anxiety is to have reminders that you can rely on when thought blocking occurs. Reminders could be bracelets, anxiety candles, essential oils, create an anxiety plan and maybe learning some mindfulness activities that work for you. Mindfulness activities are deep breathing (Square/box breathing, progressive relaxation, belly breathing, simple breathing), yoga, meditation (Guided), or structure your day with positive task.

ESSENTIAL OILS

ANXIETY CANDLE

REMINDER BRACELETS

YOU GOT THIS!

Anxiety Tool kit available at:

MADDTHERAPY.com

Anxiety tool kit contains:
Anxiety cards with
-5-4-3-2-1 grounding
-3 & 1 grounding
-Reminder cards of what to do to decrease anxiety
-Coping skills cards
-Selfcare cards
-Mindfulness cards
-An anxiety candle
-An essential oil
- Essential oil inhaler
-54321 reminder bracelet
-Chakra/Lava stone bracelet
- (2) Breathing whistle w/ case & cleaning brush
- (4) Reusable ice cubes
-Affirmation cards

Thank you for your PURCHASE

Tell us what you thought of the book on our Facebook or instagram page and receive a anxiety tool for free.

 /maddtherapy

Appendix

Active Grounding Countdown Method

NAME **5** things you	NAME **4** things you	NAME **3** things you	NAME **2** things you	NAME **1** thing you

See	feel	hear	smell	taste

Active Grounding Colors & Shapes Method

Step #1: Pick 1 color

Step #2: Name everything in the room that is that color

Step #3: Pick a 2nd color

Step #4: Name everything in the room that is that color

Step #5: Pick a 3rd color

Step #6: Name everything in the room that is that color

Step #7: Pick 1 shape

Step #8: Name everything in the room that is that shape

Now try a coping skill...

Triangle Breathing

As you breathe in you breathe in stating I am feeling calm you breathe out stating I am releasing my anxiety you breathe in new energy you breathe out releasing worries

Square Breathing

As you breathe in you breathe in stating I am feeling calm you breathe out stating I am releasing my anxiety you breathe in new energy you breathe out releasing worries

Infinity Breathing

Trace the infinity with your finger

**Remember:
In through the nose
and
out through your mouth.**

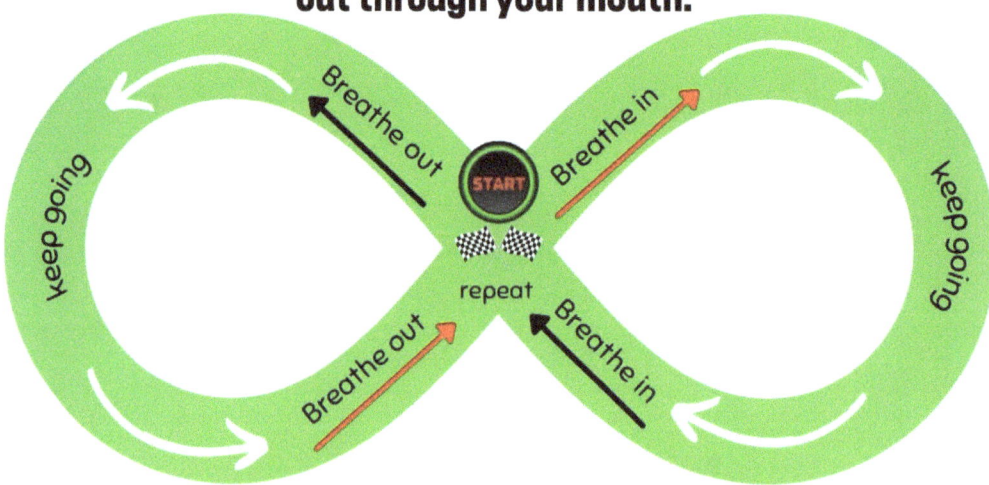

As you breathe in you breathe in stating I am feeling calm you breathe out stating I am releasing my anxiety you breathe in new energy you breathe out releasing worries

Bonus

Living in Fear of Excellence

Podcast Live - Ep. Living in Fear of Excellence
with Wesley Morgan, LPC & Keisha McDonald

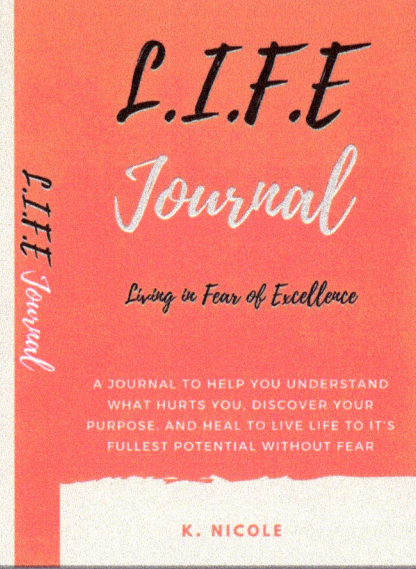

07.50   10.00

STREAMING NOW
EVERYTHING RENEWED

SCAN THE CODE TO LISTEN

Your mental health matters

PAUSE, I AM NOT MY ANXIETY

Author: Keisha McDonald
Page count: 44 pages
Publisher: AmourLegaci Publishing
Language: English
Format: Paperback
Available on: **Amazon, Barnes&Noble, AmourLegaci.com**
For Bulk orders contact AmourLegaci Publishing

Paperback:
978-1-955234-14-6

Highlights:
- Emotion Regulation
- Anxiety Education
- Feelings & Emotions
- Selfcare
- Grounding techniques
- Coping Skills

Anxiety affects not only our emotional state but also our daily life. You should never feel like you have to suffer in silence. Seek help if you are struggling with symptoms.

Keisha McDonald, MS, MA, LPC
**AUTHOR, ENTREPRENUER, THERAPIST, TRAINER
AMOURLEGACI.COM**

✉ AMOURLEGACIPUBLISHING@GMAIL.COM
f FACEBOOK.COM/AMOURLEGACI
☎ 6163172710

Parenting the Storm: A Parent's Guide to Helping Your Child Regulate

available on Amazon and Barnes & Noble

www.ingramcontent.com/pod-product-compliance
Lightning Source LLC
Chambersburg PA
CBHW061201070526
44579CB00009B/95